Let Go
of the
Load

SONJA P. DAVIS

Let Go
of the
Load

CITI OF
BOOKS

CITIOFBOOKS, INC.
3736 Eubank NE Suite A1
Albuquerque, NM 87111-3579
www.citiofbooks.com
Hotline: 1 (877) 389-2759
Fax: 1 (505) 930-7244

Ordering Information:
Quantity Sales. Special discounts are available on quantity purchases by corporations, associations, and others. For details, contact the publisher at the address above.

Printed in the United States of America.

ISBN-13		
	Paperback	978-1-959682-49-3
	eBook	978-1-959682-50-9
	Hardback	978-1-959682-63-9

Library of Congress Control Number: 2022922633

Table of Contents

DEDICATION

Everybody will face a difficult situation; it does not matter which person.

I dedicate this book to you; get armed and ready when the curveball strikes.

INTRODUCTION

Have you ever been struck by a curveball? Are you facing any life-altering negative events? Any disabilities; a severe medical condition; mental illness; death of a spouse, child, parent, or close friend; divorce; marital separation; drug or alcohol addiction; unemployment; retirement; bankruptcy; evictions; foreclosure; imprisonment. Surely, there's still hope for the future. As I let go of the load, sharing some of my experiences, might be what you need to release and thrive, even in adversity. Don't be surprised when the curveball strikes. How well will you respond?

Sometimes bad things happen to good people. Some suffering may be the result caused by your own making. You can be the best, brightest, and most faithful person. If not yet, just keep on living, life will throw you a curveball for no reason and no explanation.

What are you going to do when faced with hurdles of adversity, it comes out of nowhere, hitting you in the face, punching you in the gut, knocking you down on your knees, or maybe smacking you completely down, facing the ground. When adversity strikes me I questioned God "Why" after receiving the medical report results. Your spouse, whom you plan to spend the rest of your life with, suddenly diagnosed with a terminal illness. Your child is sick suffering from an addiction, maybe developed a rare illness from birth, or being bullied at school and later found died from gun violence or committed suicide. Your aging parents losing their minds, you are the caregiver, become overwhelmed with the truth, and they now need 24-hour care. Company downsizing unexpectedly, you were let go or still working hoping to retire, but remain due to the utilities, gasoline, health expenses, and food prices keeps going up.

Are these issues overwhelming you? How would you know God is a healer if you had never been sick? How would you know God is a provider, a way maker, a deliverer, a protector, a heart fixer, and a mind regulator if you never experience needing Him to be any of these things? Still, we question God. "Why God? Why me? Why my husband? Why my wife? Why my child? Why my job? Now my parents? It doesn't make any sense, what have I done? Help me to understand. I can't eat and I can't sleep. I am so tired. Show me what to do. This load is too much for me.

Satan, the real enemy has attacked all of us. To tame that Beast is with the Word of God. Our weapon. The Word will work if you work it. A defensive and offensive tool. You can hit a bull's eye with it. God's Word gives me hope and confidence. I share His goodness with others, so they may share, His amazing grace with someone else. With understanding, God's Word is His Will providing an abundance of His promises. Only by seeking Him, we can test His promises. They never fail. When we pray according to His Will, we will have the confidence to receive what we asked for and "Be joyful always" (1 Thess. 5:16 NIV). God listens to every prayer no matter how insignificant or mundane they appear to be. We are to wholeheartedly cast ourselves on His good graces and tender mercies. "You may ask me for anything in my name, and I will do it" (John 14:14).

NO MORE MUSCLES

Are you feeling overburdened? "Be encouraged no matter what's going on, He'll make it all right. But you got to stay strong. I know right now it's impossible to see, but God is gonna work it out if you just believe" (William Becton & Friends).

Instead of carrying that heavy load on your own, turn to God. Be encouraged to "put it all in His hands; this and that". Go ahead, turn it over to God. "He can handle it; that's a fact. He's the Master of them all". Yes, "I put it all in His hands" (Charles Hayes).

I received strength listening to Gospel lyrics, and writing in my journal became very therapeutic when a curveball knocked the air out of me. One morning in 2015, I lost my ability to walk. I was getting out of bed, and going to the bathroom to get my day started. I took a step lost my balance and fell smacked down onto the floor. I got back up, but I kept on falling. I just couldn't walk. Therefore, I ended up using a wheelchair my girlfriend had in her garage. At that moment, this social butterfly became a Wheelchair diva. In it to win it. Afterward, I made an appointment to find out what went wrong, because I had back surgery approximately 3 months ago.

After running several Blood tests, an Electromyography (EMG), MRI, a muscle Biopsy, and several consultations with three Neurologists for an expert opinion. I was later diagnosed with "Polymyositis". An aggressive medical plan was developed preparing me to be independent and up walking in approximately 18 months. Certainly, they were very clear, that it was hard to determine how much muscle weakness the inflammatory disease may have caused. Furthermore, I understood, my walk would not be the same, but at least I will be up walking.

Polymyositis is an inflammatory disease that affects skeletal muscles and those involved with making movement closer to the center of the body on both sides of the body. The causation is unknown. Neurologists think that polymyositis may be related to or triggered by a virus or an autoimmune reaction. An autoimmune reaction is when the body attacks its own tissues. An allergic response that causes irritation and muscle damage. It most often happens to people ages 31 to 60. However, I was 55, and my muscles became irritated and inflamed. They eventually started to break down causing weakness, inability to stand, trouble climbing stairs, lifting my arms, reaching out, and getting out of a chair.

Polymyositis is a rare muscle disease. Signs and symptoms usually develop gradually over weeks or months, because it is constantly undiagnosed and overlooked. According to the most recent analysis from the Myositis Association (TMA) patients reported that it takes 3 and 1/2 years and nearly five doctors to receive a correct autoimmune disease diagnosis. There is a great deal of DAMAGE DONE to the muscles during this wait time. I had related symptoms for 3 years before my doctor mentioned anything to me about Myositis.

Bringing public awareness of the disease increases positive patient outcomes. They say there is no cure, but the symptoms can be managed. I will remain hopeful that a cure for the cause gets discovered real soon. However, some treatments can improve muscle strength and function. The earlier treatment starts the more effective it is. You may need more than one kind of treatment. And your treatment may need to change over time. Treatments include steroid medicines and immunosuppressive medicines. The one I take is Immune Globulin Intravenous Gammaplex (IVIG). These are medicines that block or slow down your body's immune system. Plus, physical therapy, heat therapy, and rest. There are special devices that can help support you such as a cane or walker, but I'm limited to a wheelchair my form of support.

Polymyositis was hard for me to accept. I had just remarried 2 years prior and was in a wonderful relationship before becoming disabled. Suddenly, my husband is now my caregiver. Nevertheless, I still feel the love that flows between us. That's intimacy on another level. You

2

haven't had true love until you actually have to take care of your loved one. Ensuring all their needs are met. It's not always about sex. It's having that GENTLE TOUCH when being bathed, or when you are rubbed down with some massage oil and lotion, massaging you all over your body not missing a beat, and feeling that warm embrace when he wraps you in those nice muscular arms. That's when the passion comes. You never felt so good. Then you start appreciating and becoming grateful for the gift God places right in front of you caring for you. I feel the love of God in my heart. I treasure each moment feeling valued and worthy. These tender experiences bring me lasting joy, I do not take it for granted. Often, things messed with my mind. I didn't want to go anywhere or do anything making it rough being in a wheelchair. I just wanted to be left alone to deal with this difficult situation the best way I could.

What do you do, when you don't know what to do? Do you need something that seems so impossible that only God can handle? I began praying & praising expecting some type of miracle from a supernatural God who's able to do unexplainable things. Decide to praise God when facing adversities. Within adversity lies opportunity. Praise moves God to intervene when we feel completely trapped in difficult situations.

God not only has ultimate power over all things, but He is also the source of our power. God can do the impossible. There is nothing too hard for Him. He can take nothing and turn it into something. He can make a way when there seems to be no other way. He can heal the sick. Raise the dead. Feed the hungry. Clothing naked. He lay down His life, didn't anybody take it? He was crucified and resurrected. He'll give you double for your trouble. His angels will protect us. He provides shelter during a storm. He loves us unconditionally. He's always with us and never left us. When He speaks things change. God can speak light into your darkest hour, and speak hope to hopeless situations and broken dreams. God is in control and He is faithful. Stay focused on God and not the problem. Remind God of His promises and watch Him work. "Do not be afraid. Stand firm and you will see the deliverance the Lord will bring you today. The Lord will fight for you; you need only to be still" (Ex. 14:13-14 NIV).

On occasion I found myself having to remind my husband of our wedding vows. And stressed, "I'm to love you if you stay with me, and I'm strong enough to survive you if you leave me". He insisted that he wasn't going anywhere and he was going to take care of me because he loves me. He misses the way we used to be. And I do too. However, his ways and his actions speak louder than his words. Often in relationships, problems arise because of our expectations of others. We must let go of these expectations and accept people as they are. With that said, I will stay in peace, which is a position of power, and let God deal with my husband. God operates secretly and quietly, but surely. Stand still and see the deliverance the Lord will bring. He will intentionally become involved in your situation. "And we know that in all things God works for the good of those who love Him, who have been called according to His purpose (Rom 8:28 NIV).

This adversity caused me to draw closer to God. With a legacy of faith, I must give credit to my parents, especially my mother who played a significant role and influence in my spiritual development. In the meantime, I must stay armed for this battle. I discovered that I am able to deal with things I cannot control. When you fix your eyes on Jesus and not on your circumstances, you will begin to see life differently. God can work through every situation in your life even the one you are facing right now to bring you closer to Himself.

Furthermore, when adversity strikes you must get your fight back. Letting go of my load led me to the Word of God. It gives you the power to fight the Beast you have within. God stands by His Word that's full of Rock Solid promises. Many involve granting peace. And He's faithful to fulfill every last one of His promises.

Get back in the ring, trust God, and go on the 12 rounds with Him. Undoubtedly, we will win. For every setback, God already has a comeback. For every disappointment He has restoration. But for every injustice He has vindication. For the betrayal that seems to be working against you, God knows how to turn around and cause it to work for your good. Above all, do not let pride or arrogance stop you from praising and worshiping God. It doesn't matter who you are.

The blow of having Polymyositis staggered us once more, with the insurance company denying "Rituximab" a medication that was part of the Neurologist's medical plan. They thought it had a positive effect on my medical condition and functional ability. Although, Rituximab is a covered drug by the Food and Drug Administration (FDA) for treating Cancer not Myositis (my diagnosis). It's considered experimental and experimental drugs are not covered under my health insurance policy. We appealed their decision, but later received another denial. How could this be? Another curveball! That one punched me in the face, head, and heart. The enemy is really trying to knock me out.

Don't stay down when life hits you with something difficult. The battle is not for us to fight alone. God wouldn't have brought me to this moment if it wasn't a purpose for it. When all hell is breaking loose its time to be still and know He is God. Sometimes in the plan of God, things get worse before they get better. God is with us even when there is no evidence of His presence. We become empowered when we start praying, praising, and thanking God for the strength to get back up even in the most difficult situations. We are never alone. He will see you through. What's more, He can do the impossible. For instance, healing me without ever taking the medication because I am destined to win. "No weapon formed against me shall be able to prosper" (Isa 54:17 NKJV).

With that being said, I decided not to worry but trust. Not to keep being upset, but content. I glanced into my rearview mirror and saw how God made a way for me in the past. He did it before. He would do it again. Suddenly, I felt the presence of God, the Calmer of every storm all around me. I was no longer afraid anymore. I had confidence that I will receive God's grace and His mercy. Having a touch of His favor in the land of the living. With faith, I see the glory of God in all things. When I believe I feel Divine energy swelling within me. Trusting that everything will be all right, even though I don't see any evidence of it. Then Jesus said, "Did I not tell you that if you believed, you will see the glory of God?" (John 11:40 NIV).

Everybody will go through something that will bring you down to your knees. You need a friend who will stick with you through the bad times, someone who will pray for you uplifting your spirit reminding you that better days are coming. "'A righteous man have many troubles but the Lord delivers him from them all" (Ps 34:19 NIV).

Let Go of The Load. Unleash the pain within. That cup of pain is not enough to keep you down. God can keep you from falling. Sometimes you have to cry while releasing unhealthy feelings, opinions, and negative thinking. Most importantly, you must have a renewed mind in order to receive some Godly peace. It is the presence of joy in unhappiness. A person who has genuine Godly peace, can endure an avalanche of hardship and difficulty and still enjoy an inner peace that surpasses all human understanding.

Throughout this book, you will become encouraged, entertained, and uplifted. You will be inspired and amazed knowing we can handle any situation we face because there is absolutely nothing too hard for God. There is no such thing as life without pain and suffering. Situations will come in our lives that will knock us down time after time. However, we don't have to stay down, have the mindset of a fighter to get back up again with the power, confidence, and strength to knock that Beast's head off.

Anyone that needs to be restored and feel all hope is gone. Keep the faith. Keep believing. Keep trusting. We serve a God that can do anything but fail. Choose to focus on God and not your problems. No matter what is going on in your life. Keep standing on the Promises of God. He is behind the scene and working things out for our good.

"I am just a nobody trying to tell everybody about somebody who can save anybody" (The Williams Brothers).

FAITH AND FEAR

What are you waiting for God to do on your behalf?
How are you using your faith?
Can you wait by faith?
Are you dwelling on the negative?
Are you expecting the worst?

Job 3:25 (NIV) states "What I feared has come upon me; what I dreaded has happened to me."

Fear cannot stay where faith is, and faith doesn't mature and strengthens without trials. Each trial becomes a stepping-stone to a stronger and deeper faith. Likewise, when put the right actions with expectancy, you put your faith to work. You begin to prepare while waiting on God. As you grow in faith, you start to "feed off" stuff the enemies throw at you. As a result, you become stronger.

Some days, it was hard getting started with having a mustard seed of faith. Yet, I wouldn't give up. Standing firm in the faith, I replace negative thoughts with positive ones. Once I renewed my thinking, I became unstoppable.

At some point, we have to release the pressure that is weighing us down. Like any damaged product you must return it to the manufacturer for repairs. Just because you had a beatdown, doesn't mean you won't have a great turnaround. There is a purpose for the pain. In the book of James chapter one reminds us to "Consider it pure joy, my brothers and sisters, whenever you face trials of many kinds, because you know that the testing of your faith develops perseverance. Perseverance must finish its work so that you may be mature and complete, lacking nothing."

I know firsthand the burdens you carry can be too much to bear. I lost hope when I couldn't walk on my own. Then I developed a fear of falling. So I had to get my mind right, and started reading Psalms 23 "He leads me beside quiet waters, He refreshes my soul. He guides me along the right paths; even though I walk through the darkest valley I will fear no evil for He is with me. His rod and His staff comfort me. It's through those VALLEY experiences you can see the Hand of God operating in your life. When conflicting thoughts enter my mind, I start writing putting my pain to paper to hold on to my faith and receive that unspeakable joy back into my life.

Writing is extremely therapeutic for me. Instead of thinking negatively, I have pure thoughts that honored Jesus and later received that JOY I was seeking through my writing. I continue to push through some private pain others have experienced. I tempt to address and find the root of problems that sometimes gets ignored. I realize how important prayer is and how it changes things and people too.

Therefore, I would use my words as tools to lift bow down heads and up the spirits. A vessel of love God uses to touch His people. Instead of WORDS AS WEAPONS to bring people down. I want to be a blessing. I want to encourage someone who has lost their way burdened with so much pain. I wanted to take my words to enrich your life as you grow in love with Jesus. Our gracious Heavenly Father will relieve you from carrying that heavy load. It is not His will for us to be burdened down. He wants to provide, comfort, strengthen, love, and use us in unexpected ways. "Cast your burden on the Lord, and He will sustain you" (Ps 55:22 ESV). "Come to me, all you who are weary and burdened, and I will give you rest". (Matt 11:28 NIV).

As I Rise through pain, my scars are the driving force to keep me moving forward. Regardless, of what you're going through pray until something happens (PUSH) through it no matter what your situation is we have to learn to remain calm during a storm. You can overcome adversities, and recover from difficulties and circumstances that have come against you. Bend through it. Rise above it. Don't give up FAITH WORKS put it into action. Don't let what you feel affect what you say, because you will receive what you believe. Don't let what is temporarily become a permanent fixture in your life. You got this hang in there until your change comes.

My journey enables me to roll alongside you, because of my tear-stained path, giving you this SPECIAL TOUCH of comfort to ease your pain. At first, I've got disappointed due to fear and lack of faith. Yet, I knew God was with me and I should trust Him, but I still feel terrified. However, working through my emotions led me to an aha moment. Forget about your feelings and have faith in God. Faith is the connector that connects us with the power and blessings of God. All we have to do is believe and speak His Word. One word from God can change everything for you. It can heal you and deliver you from private pain.

One day, while patiently waiting to have physical therapy. An Earthly Angel sits down right beside me. She looked at me, reached out, and held both my hands. Immediately, she started praying for me. Then she encouraged me to stay strong and not to give up. She explained that God loves me and He hears me when I pray. He sees everything I'm going through and reassured me, that everything is going to be all right. I have to keep hope alive. And she advised me to keep believing and trusting in God.

I had placed more importance on the medical report instead of focusing on God, my Healer; my Deliverer; my Provider; and my Protector. I receive peace knowing that He is with me, regardless of the outcome. I know you want the pain to go away, but the affliction serves a purpose. I know it is very hard to recognize purpose in your affliction. Nevertheless, my affliction led me to my purpose, and my purpose is bigger than my pain.

Furthermore, God knows what we need before we even ask, nothing is hidden from Him. "Taste and see that the Lord is good. Blessed is the one who takes refuge in Him" (Ps 34:8 NIV). When we get a taste of God working in our lives, we are more prepared to wait with expectations for His plan for us to unfold. In November 2018, without ever receiving the Rituximab, Polymyositis went into remission. God blessed me, regardless. Rituximab was not part of God's plan He had for me. Proverbs 3:5-6 states "Trust in the Lord with all your heart, and lean not on your own understanding; in all your ways acknowledge him, and he will make your paths straight." We are to trust and obey God leaving all the consequences to Him. Every problem we face has its solution found in the Word of God. Now, my muscles can recover on their own. Surely, I believe God can restore and make them strong again. All He wants us to do is to remain faithful and trust Him. He delights in meeting our needs physically, emotionally, and spiritually.

Within these pages are loads of difficult situations being released. To inspire and encourage you to lay your burdens down, so you can embrace God's protective presence. The contents deliver a message of HOPE and hopefully, a tool that leads you to feast on the Word of God. The source of our strength.

This book is my gift to you "Let Go of The Load" Keep it close dear friend!

THE CAREGIVERS

Do you assist with personal care?
Are you patient?
Are you dependable, and trustworthy?
Would someone criticize you as a caregiver?

There are times when stress and frustration come from having to depend on others, especially family members who are full-time caregivers. They get fatigued and burn out. That affects not just yourself, but the person you care for. This worse their capacity for compassion. Likewise, by adding clashing personalities to the mix, conflicts are almost bound to happen. How you respond depends on the situation. "A gentle answer turns away wrath, but a harsh word stirs up anger" (Proverbs 15:1 NIV)

There are times when I feel that I'm held captive by fear, burdens, and frustration. It is doing those times that I have to remind myself to seek strength and encouragement through praying and connecting with Jesus. That's when I ask the Lord to help me to dig deep to replace negativity with positive thoughts, and to trust Him to see me through. Therefore, my role as the person receiving the care chooses to offer genuine praise. Making it very clear how much I appreciate the caregiving to me. Recognizing that their bucket may feel empty at times, and needs replenishing. I make it my business to practice compassion allowing them to vent when they feel overwhelmed because holding in feelings can result in growing frustration.

A full-time caregiver should be placed on a pedestal for all the work it takes to care for someone. But there are times when caregivers become mean, grouchy, evil, and have a nasty attitude, because they're really tired of taking care of you, neglecting things they need to do and want to do for themselves. With that said, let the roles be reversed. Give out the same treatment. Sort of reaping what you sow. Maybe, the caregivers would start being more empathetic, kind-hearted, and compassionate.

Anyway, I am very much aware caregivers need to receive love, appreciation, and encouragement too. I am truly grateful for my family. All is well, so I smile, even though I have been through it for a while, still, I smile, knowing that God is behind the scenes working things out for my good. Surely, this too shall pass, but it would be great if it happens now. At that moment I began to pray.

"Father, thank You for Your grace and mercy. Thank You for Your favor and for withholding deserve punishment. Instead, You blessed me with the care I need, keeping me in my right mind while disabled and limited to a wheelchair. I know you see the struggles in my heart. Sometimes that I pain, I know I need to let go and hand them over to you. And not make the mistake of feasting on my problems, making them bigger than you. Therefore, I choose to unfasten, release and let go of the struggles that I do not understand. "I will be glad and rejoice in your unfailing love, for you have seen my troubles, and you care about the anguish of my soul" (Ps 31:7 NLT). Oh, how comforting to know that when TROUBLE COMES You are my safe place." My refuge and strength, an ever-present help in times of trouble" (Psalms 46:1 NLT). The place I go when I'm fearful or full of anxiety and need peace, I found it in Your Word. In Jesus' Name, Amen!

Life is going to throw us curveballs. They cannot be avoided. Embrace them to see how they can make your life better. We might not understand everything that's going on in our lives, but God has a plan for every problem and turn it around, and use it to bring us good because He loves us. Remember, the trials we face are temporary and only for a season. We have seen God's goodness, faithfulness, and fingerprints working for us in the past. He has more than we can ever imagine, ask, or think about in our future. We must wait patiently for God to enter into our situations. Waiting is not one of my strongest suits, but the outcome is well worth the wait. The appointed time is the best time. God's timing is perfect and always right on time. Stay in faith. Keep doing the right thing. Obey God and only trust Him. He is faithful and true to His Word.

REMEMBERING 2009

In the world of Horsing Racing consider me as a Longshot. Don't count me out and without a doubt, include me in your exotic bets. I believe I can do this because I've been set apart for a specific purpose. Predetermined by God, before being born, that I am destined to win. Therefore, meet me in the winner's circle!

In 2009, I went from cheering and giving out high-fives to wailing and receiving many condolences. That year, a long shot named "Mine That Bird" pulled off an upset winning the most famous race, the Kentucky Derby. Also, the last Derby was spent with my Dad. Furthermore, in the same year, my marriage reached its breaking point. And lastly, it was the same year when the "King of Pop" Michael Jackson, died.

As I let go of the load-releasing pain held within, I recall years of celebrating the Kentucky Derby with my parents. One year particularly 2009, which would be the last year with my Dad. He passed later that year on the 28th day of September. Derby was a special occasion for my parents. It was their tradition to have guests over to prepare for the big Kentucky Derby race called the "Run For The Roses". Mama & Daddy would prepare a fabulous breakfast. It consists of bacon, sausage, scrambled eggs, creamy slow-cooked grits, fried potatoes and onions, fried apples, jelly, apple butter, biscuits, and the aroma of a fried Rabbit smelling like Kentucky Fried Chicken smothered in gravy filled the kitchen. Including, orange juice and grapefruit juice. We often laughed about grapefruit juice. Supposedly, it burns up all the fat we just ate. Who wouldn't want to continue that tradition?

After that hearty breakfast, it was time to fire up the grill for Daddy's amazing Baby Back Ribs; turned a three-car garage; the backyard; and the patio into a nightclub. Then we started wiring up speakers for music and a big-screen TV. Most importantly, stocking ingredients for Mint Juleps (Derby's signature drink) along with bottles of Woodford Reserve and other Top-shelf liquors and placing beer on ice in coolers.

Before placing our bets, we would go relax in the living room, my brother, Dad and I to discuss the Horse Racing Experts betting picks and predictions. Here's a load drop: My Dad was a professional gambler. He taught us well. Besides, he and his cousin were Bookies. They accepted and placed bets and paid out winnings. Therefore, along with pen and paper, we have on hand a racing form (horses info), scratch sheet (lists the horses withdrawn from that day's race, along with the betting odds and statistics for the horses) and the sports section of the newspaper to read stories about every racehorse running in the Derby race at Churchill Downs on the first Saturday in May.

It was important to know the weatherman's predictions. If it's likely to rain, you would look for a horse that runs well on a muddy track; have the best speed; include your favorite jockey; has a great trainer that has a good Longshot based on previous races, or has the heart to win. Daddy explained to me not to underestimate a Longshot. Always include them in your exotic bets because there's a purpose for being in the race. They have a chance of winning. Don't count them out. If one hits the board at the finish line. Expect a big payday. Finally, we have our top four picks destined to win.

Now the guests begin to arrive with excitement. The Derby party is now in full swing. The horses are now headed to their gates. We're waiting patiently for the Derby race to begin. And now they're off, running one and 1/4 miles around the track to get to the Finish Line. The anticipation got excited, and everybody up yelling for their horses to reach the finish line. Here it comes down the stretch on the inside rail a Longshot at 50-1 odds "Mine That Bird" with my Dad's favorite jockey, Calvin Borel. The horse paid $103.20 to win on a $2 bet. YAY, we won! I'm a winner baby. All you need is a little bit of faith when the odds are stacked against you. With determination and God's help, you will win.

That was considered a ritual to come to my parent's house for Derby. Everybody came by. The neighborhood, our family, and friends. I mean everybody. I didn't realize that would be the last Derby I would spend with my Dad. My parents will forever be remembered for their Derby parties. Those times together gave me sweet memories and moments that shine like diamonds in my mind. Jewels I will always cherish. Lord, thank You for the wonderful memories that bring me joy. John 16:20 states "You will grieve, but your grief will turn to joy."

Furthermore, in 2009, my marriage fell apart soon after burying my Dad. That being my third marriage, it's not for everyone. Here's a load dropped; especially, married to a mama's boy. Another curveball. When we started dating I noticed the strong connections he had with his mom, and that won me over. I felt my husband's relationship with his mom would be beneficial for everyone. However, those feelings turned into resentment, after what I said or what I wanted didn't matter. Therefore, it became very hard to remain peaceful, when boundaries were crossed. Divorce inevitable. I know I'm strong enough to survive a man. I know who I am and whose I am. Plus, I recall an old saying "If you love someone set him free, if he comes back to you he's yours, if not, it was never meant to be."

After a couple of years, he realized I was the best woman he ever had, even his mama told him that. She and I had developed a beautiful relationship. He realized that he needed me, and wanted me back in his life. With the understanding of 1 Corinthians 13:4-7 "Love is patient, love is kind. It does not envy, it does not boast, it is not proud. It does not dishonor others, it is not self-seeking, it is not easily angered, and it keeps no record of wrongs. Love does not delight in evil but rejoices with the truth. It always protects, always trusts, always hopes, always perseveres."

Later, in 2012 while attending church, we rekindled our relationship. That led us to remarry in 2013 for the second time around. One morning we got up and decided to get married. So, we went to the courthouse, had a romantic lunch at home, and got back in bed listening to the O'Jays. We've been together ever since with a mutual understanding of what love is not." I am no one's shadow. I need my very own spot to stand" (Gladys Knight). I am secure in whom God created me to be. I'm going to let my light shine.

HOT AND HOLY

Hey sister! Yes you, my sister, you, you, and you too. Do you have time for me? Will you make time for me? We need to talk about something my sister. There's no room for distractions this requires total focus. Allow me to scale back and let the truth flow through. If you wondering what's up, times up sister, to close those blinds my sister, the one you keep opening and closing. Awe yeah, see it, that one right there, the one in the middle with the monkey in the window, that gold mine you got, the one you keep opening and closing that what's up. You are not alone my sister. Been There Done That. Exposure brings us closer. I'm surrendering a load from the past. Here's my experience so check this out.

I flew to Bloomington, Minnesota to settle a worker's compensation case during my birthday and stayed at the Radisson Blu connected to the Mall of America. After meeting with our defense counsels, I intended to go shopping. Once I arrived back at the hotel there was a surprise at the front desk that flew in for my birthday. I was handed a dinner invitation, and while leaning forward I was told that I will be picked up at 7:00 p.m. So I went to my room to get ready for this mysterious adventure and searched for the sexist outfit I packed with me on this trip. I've always stayed ready for pleasure. Now it's time to go. Oh my, I'm lost for words. This place is amazing. I was so excited and extremely thrilled to be up in a Penthouse suite in downtown Minneapolis. Dinner was outstanding. It exceeded all of my expectations having a seductive atmosphere.

Later I was encouraged to remove my shoes, after receiving flowers, jewelry, chocolate candy, and a beautiful bottle of perfume. Teased my mind, serving some of that "Mary Jane" (weed), and drinking the

17

finest Wine. Enticed me with designer clothes, a pair of red bottom shoes, and a designer purse, which had a stack of money in it too. Also, charmed with promises of good times and prosperity. Then bribed into creating wealth and popularity. Inflamed my imagination, keeping it pumped up and calculating.

At this point, whatever I do must be done exceptionally well. Must be bold, not basic, but capable to be remembered. Confident, strong, and unforgettable. Burning with passion, I started dancing making it sexy. With great pleasure, cast a spell with my performance, had all his attention, and held on to it. He looks like he has been SAVAGED by a wild animal. The excitement was so invigorating caused a stimulating effect. He was so mesmerized it made his nature rise. The force was very irresistible. Enhance my sexuality. He suddenly had a craving for my "Vajayjay".

Begging over, and over, and over again to taste and smell these "honey lips", but kept them out of reach making him want what I had to offer. Some of this sweet and tender love. Besides, I've learned how to say what I need at the right moment to get what I want. Plus, I was told that I had a gold mine between my legs and I should never be destitute lacking nothing. His craving brought out the beast in me. So, I passionately kissed him and started dancing to show how much I desired him too.

Began doing the splits, but dropped it because we were sizzling hot. Now give me what you got! Oh how sensational, so electrifying. He thought he had me. Oh no! No! No! I never lost control. I did what needed to be done. He went where he's never gone before. It was like a pressure cooker ready to explode. Instantly, shot off like a burst of color in the sky at a fireworks display, or like a Roman candle shooting for the stars, STRICTLY BUSINESS my sister. I was focused and determined to get ahead, successfully worked on that head, earned and deserved my bread, to take care of my home. But enough is enough!

Grasping for the material and physically losing myself in the process. Being stuck, selling my soul, and not knowing what to do about it. I try running away from it but ended up running right back to the very thing, I kept running from. No matter how hard I tried, I can't fly away with just one wing. I was trying my hardest to do what was right and walk away from what is not. I became addicted and wanted more. You must be willing to stand in your truth. You don't know how strong you are until you face something ugly. But enough is enough!

Times Up and Rise! Listen to me, my sister. He thinks he has you too. Telling you to use that gold mine you got to get what you want. Now you got the booty twerking and clapping. Impressive, he never had seen a booty work like that before. Immediately, was captivated, stimulated, and aroused. I know all about that, been there and done that. Times up and rise, my sister. Start using your creative mind, and not that energetic behind. We are worth more than that. We are Treasures, something valuable, very special, classy beyond comparison, unique and wonderfully made, and so precious. Come on sister reach out take my hand, together stronger we stand, you're not alone my sister. Been there! Done that!

I know you think Dr. Feel Good satisfies all your needs. But it ain't no way to continually be on your back or down on your knees to receive what you need. Is this how a CEO leads his greatest asset? To earn your place, you got to work the head for you to get ahead, in this organization. Sisters, you must understand the seriousness of this situation. Times up! Rise up! Sister don't you know you are a primary Stakeholder? Your actions can affect the outcome of this company. You started from the bottom now you are here. Prepared, equipped, and qualified. You know how to plan, execute and have amazing results. Enough is enough! Don't tolerate things that come from the devil. Don't let it paralyze you. Within you, there's the power to overcome doubt and push past fear, guilt, and shame. Including, manipulations and intimidations. Surrender all to God. He will forgive you and restore to you everything the devil tries to take away from you. Come on my sister, reach out and take my hand, together stronger we stand, you're not alone my sister. Been there and done that now I'm free.

You see, I knew what tools I have within that made me irresistibly sexy. Therefore, for me to live lavishly and extravagantly, I had a side Hustle. Using my creative mind being a fantasy, dressing up, and entertaining charming well-established men that had it going on for themselves. They are sharp-dressing extinguished gentlemen with an intoxicating smell that attracts you like a magnet and know how to treat a lady.

Don't you dare judge me? Does my sexiness upset you? Everyone has a seductive personality trait that draws people to them. I know how to get what I want. Whenever, wherever, however, whatever I want it. Quite often men find it appealing, when a woman shows confidence, takes control, and does what needs to be done, creating an unforgettable experience. It's not always about having sex. It's having peace, relaxation, laughter, joy, and satisfaction after being in my presence. I never had any problems having to get my needs met by men and God. I was hot and holy. I enjoy creating pleasant situations and having satisfying events making things happen to watch them unfold.

Still, I went to church. Creating balance. Getting my soul lifted. I enjoy worshipping and praising God because I love Him too. I continued singing in the choir. Attending Bible study. And would pray at the altar. The Lord was making every effort to speak to me in my circumstances. Yet, I wasn't listening to what He was saying to me. I was busy having a good time. I knew something had to change. I was making some very unwise decisions, especially, the way I was being provided for by God and men. Still, my behavior needed to change. The choice is mine.

As I continue going to church being hot and holy, I began to embrace that resurrected power down inside me. The Holy Spirit was diminishing negative self-talk with faith-filled Words. "I can do all things through Christ who strengthens me" (Phil 4:13 NKJV). "Greater is He who is within me than he that's in the world" (1 John 4:4 NIV).

Please be patient with me. God is behind the scenes working things out for me. I began owning and confessing my sins without shame or embarrassment. I pray to the Lord to change my heart for a deeper understanding of His Word, which led me to turn my life around. A change came over me when I surrendered to the power of God. His Divine grace is my spiritual safety net and the assurance that no matter what I may go through, I will not go through it alone.

A transformation took place in my heart. I'm so grateful for how God changed my life. I no longer wanted to please my flesh. Instead, I yearned for God's grace and mercy. I ask Him to help me and encourage me to become the person He created me to be. I released past disappointments with a forgiving heart. My faith led me to overcome the circumstances of my past and become a woman of influence. God's the reason to be down on your knees, so you can remain on your feet. Everything I am I owe to God. Everything I have comes from God. And all belong to Him. Thank You, Lord, for being everything I need and more.

God is doing a new thing in my life. It'll be greater than I can imagine. He tells us to "Forget the former things; do not dwell on the past. See, I am doing a new thing! Now it springs up; do you not perceive it?" (Isa 43:18-19 NIV).

ADVERSE ATTITUDE

Are there any sins you committed you haven't been honest with God about?

Have you ever cheated on your tax returns?

Have you ever called in sick when you were not?

Have you ever cheated on your spouse or a significant other?

Did you tear down someone's character to make yourself look better?

Have you ever done something that seems right at the time, not intending to do any harm, but, it came back biting you in the butt?

Are you bitter about something?

Have you encountered a person who gets on your nerves?

Are you judgmental?

Are you holding a grudge?

Do you need to mind your own business?

Did you intentionally get pregnant to trap a man? What good did it do for you? What about your child?

Are you the other woman or the man? The side piece? Know your role.

Are you two-faced?

Are you selfish?

Can you have a heart for something that is not about you?

Are you arrogant?

Do you boast or brag?

Do you lack empathy toward other people?

Why do you have to lie when the truth is staring you right in your face?

In Isaiah chapter 1, provides an introduction to the issues of sin, judgment, and hoped for restoration. God confronts His people about wrongs they had committed. Even then God responded mercifully, asking the people of Judah to confess what they had done and turn from it. God is sovereign. He has supreme authority and absolute power over all things. He longs for us to be open and honest with Him. "If we confess our sins, he is faithful and just and will forgive us our sins and purify us from all unrighteousness" (1 John 1:9 NIV).

We must guard our hearts against bitterness. Release it. Bitterness will follow you everywhere you go. Here's my experience dealing with someone's bitterness... bitter people are hard to deal with and very unpleasant. They destroy relationships. Very negative. They walk around with a chip on their shoulder. They have inner hurt, and anger and carry emotions on their sleeves. They want you to read their mind. They are ruthless with sharp tongues, saying things that hurt people's feelings. They hold on to grudges and are very judgmental. "Do not judge, or you too will be judged. For in the same way you judged, and with the measure you use, it will be measured to you" (Matthew 7:1-2 NIV). We all have said unkind things and done unkind things that seem right at the time. We have been judged harshly and unfairly. We must pray, asking God to help release bitterness, anger, and unforgiveness held in our hearts. It holds you back. The Bible states "Get rid of all bitterness, rage and anger, brawling and slander, along with every form of malice. Be kind and compassionate to one another, forgiving each other, just as Christ Jesus forgave you" (Eph. 4:31-32 NIV). The Bible goes on to say "See to it that no one misses the grace of God and that no bitter root grows up to cause trouble and defile many" (Heb. 12:15 NIV). Also, Colossians 3:13 states, "Bear with each other and forgive one another, if any one of you has a grievance against someone forgive as the Lord forgave you." Consider the circumstances and not take them personally.

As I forgive, I open my mind and become willing to see things from the view of others. Instead of focusing on the negative, look for the good in them. It helps me better understand how things unfolded. We must be able to stand in our truth. Maybe, we are the ones that actually caused the conflict in the first place. Besides, what's in your heart comes out of your mouth (Matt 12:34 NIV). Let go of the load of bitterness and evil thoughts. Have a forgiving heart. Choose your words wisely. Be kind and humble. We want God's forgiveness, so we must forgive others.

Norman Vincent Peale said, "Give everyone a smile. Spend so much time improving yourself that you have no time left to criticize others. Be too big for worry and too noble for anger."

SHACKING UP

Living together and having sexual relations without being married. Also, known as fornication.

Curveball: It's not a good idea to be shaking up. It doesn't end well.

I was shacking up with my boyfriend, who was a gangster. He was 10 years older than me. Therefore, being married to him never entered my mind. Although he was fun and charming, he wasn't someone I wanted to spend the rest of my life with. Still, I was attracted to a bad boy, who was confident and brave. He never backed down from any challenge. I felt protective and thrilled to be by his side. He never let anyone push him around. He ran things the way he wanted. He called the shots, while others did what he told them to do. My parents never liked him. The more they talked about him the more I wanted to be with him.

This relationship was fantastic, at first. He is very romantic. He paid all the bills and would buy me anything my heart desired. I worked and saved my money. We lived the life of luxury. We took vacations. Drove nice cars. Lived in a beautiful home. Wore designer clothes and shoes. And he made sure I carry only designer purses, that had a loaded 357 Magnum Revolver inside. He shows me how to use it. Insisted that I packed it, because of the lifestyle he lived.

Can you believe that someone you love, who claims to love you would verbally, mentally, and physically abuse you? Have you ever been out in public embarrassed, after being humiliated, and yelled at in front of people? Have you ever been manipulated by someone who played on your emotions and made you feel guilty? Did you ever leave the relationship and find yourself returning because the sex was so good?

I was addicted to the emotional roller coaster. It had a magnetic pull on me. We shacked up for 5 years before the abuse started. One day, out of the blue, he began accusing me of flirting with other men. Then became extremely jealous when I would go out with my girlfriends. He would even get ticked off, if I stayed too long visiting my parents. He was trying to control me. Constantly calling me and dropping by my job, unexpectedly. The more he drank and did lines of cocaine, the angrier he gets, so the fighting begins. We will break up, then here he comes back crying, begging, and apologizing saying, ''I'm sorry, but you made me do it. That'll never happen again. You know I love you. I will never put my hands on you again, I'm so sorry." Often, he will use gifts, sex, and money for me to forgive him and let him back in. So, I did.

Therefore, we were doing great for quite a while, until one day somebody made him mad, so he takes it out on me. That happened on several occasions. I finally had enough. I wasn't taking it anymore. I wanted out of the relationship. He hit me one time too many. I'm packing up my kids and we're leaving. He became very angry, trying to bully me around, when I attempted to leave. He said, "If you leave, I'm going to kill you." So, I stayed until he went to sleep. Then, I gathered some clothes for me and the kids, put them in the car before waking them up. I call myself sneaking back in, but he had already gotten up, sniffing a line of cocaine. Then he grabbed me, punched and slapped me in the face, busting my lip. He took the gun off the dresser, pointed it towards my head, pulling the trigger, but the loaded gun jammed. It encountered a malfunction. It misfires.

What happened simply amazes me. God sent His Angel to save me. He shut the mouth of that gun. I must give glory to God, the gun jammed. It didn't shoot. Thank You Lord for Your promises of protection. My God, whom I will always trust, provided me with a way of escape. Praise the Lord! That was Divine Intervention. I was miraculously saved from what could have been death. It pays to have a relationship with a God who saves. We can deepen our faith when we understand that God has ways we can't even imagine.

At that point, I became empowered. Although my gun was in my purse, I couldn't get to it, so I ran into the kitchen, got an iron skillet, and started swinging it, hitting him and beating him with it. Then got a hold of my straightening comb, threw it at him, and struck him across his back. He staggered and fell on the floor. I was able to get some more licks in. Kicking his ass. Meanwhile, I grabbed up my kids and ran next door waking up my neighbors who called the police. When they arrived, they saw evidence of me being in a fight, because I had a black eye and a busted lip. It was suggested that I go to the hospital, but I refuse to go. The police followed us home, but he had already gone.

Later, I had the locks changed and took out an Emergency Protection Order (EPO). So, when the police catch him, they will lock him up. A few days later, he came back, beating on my door. Mad as hell, because I had the locks changed. I dialed 911, he was gone of course when the police arrived. This went on for quite a while. I moved around from pillar to post, no matter where I go, he seems to always find me.

At the time, nobody knew what I was going through. I was too embarrassed to say anything, to anyone. Until one Sunday after church, heading to my car, in the church parking. I noticed my car windows have been busted out. I was so humiliated and embarrassed. The police were contacted and took a report. It was obvious my car was targeted, being the only vehicle severely damaged. I was asked, " if I was having problems with anybody". At that point, I told them about the EPO taken out on my ex-boyfriend. I told them it's been a complete nightmare, he's been stalking and torturing me.

That incident agonized me for days wondering what will happen the next time he decided to do something. He kept calling me at work. It affected my productivity. I began losing weight. My hair was falling out. My nerves were shot. My kids didn't understand what was going on with me.

Finally, I got tired of running and very tired of being called a Gypsy. Because I moved a lot, running and hiding from him. It didn't matter that the police were called. He always got away. So one day, I had made up my mind, I wasn't running anymore. I started thinking about the times he hit me, cursed at me, bullied me, stalked me, threatened, humiliated, embarrassed, and intimidated me. Ignited a fire inside me. I wasn't taking it anymore. I cried out to the Lord, "Father, give me strength to defeat this devil. I can't do it on my own, but I know You can. I'm trusting You to take care of me. You have done it before, I know You can do it again." I'd made up my mind, that I was going to use what he brought me for protection from him. I'm going to give him a piece of steel. Everything he taught me, about aiming and shooting, I was going to use on him. In my mind, I believe that I was a sharpshooter. I was determined not to miss my target.

Early one morning, I was leaving to drop the kids off at the babysitter's house before going to work. He pulled into the driveway blocking me in, so I couldn't leave. I don't know what he came here to do. But the Bible says "No weapon formed against you shall prosper" (Isa. 54:17). God protects me from danger seen and unseen.

Therefore, he's yelling at me saying, "You ain't going nowhere." Two weeks prior he'd got arrested. So, we went to court over the EPO. He was told not to contact me, and to stay so many feet away from me. If not, he would be serving time in jail. However, that didn't matter to him, because he served time before for illegal gambling and selling drugs.

Anyways, he gets out of his car cursing at me. So, I get out of my car pointing my gun at him saying "Move your car I got to go to work". I am telling the kids to "get down in the back seat." I said to him, "I dare you to take another step. Your family will be burying you". He saw I wasn't playing, so I continue saying "I am not afraid of you. I'm not running or hiding from you. And most definitely, I don't want you in my life anymore! I moved on! Leave me alone!" So he said " So it's like that now. You want to shoot me? You really don't want me anymore." I said, "No, sure don't want you." Now get the hell away from here. You're making me late." Then he left saying, " I leave you alone. I'm not going to bother you." It was finally over. He never bothered me again.

With help from the Lord, I was able to look at that devil straight in the eyes being fearless. Displaying strength and showing him, that he had no more power over me. Women who are abused are more likely to develop anxiety and thoughts of killing their abuser. Abuse of any kind is wrong. Don't accept it. No matter what. Make a decision that you want better for yourself. Surrender that abuse over to the Lord and let Him heal your heart.

Here's a beautiful prayer from Devon Franklin that blessed me, let it encourage you:

"Dear Lord, I accept that there are things I've had to endure that I may never understand. I ask You for healing emotionally, mentally, physically, and spiritually. Please give me comfort in the times when discomfort is the only feeling available to me. I accept that You have created me for greatness, and I commit myself to pursue it every day. I accept that some men cannot handle all you have created me to be. But I will not make myself smaller to fit into their limited view of who I am! I no longer accept any man who can't respect me! I no longer accept anyone who tries to make me feel inferior! I no longer accept feelings of insecurity or lack of self-worth! I accept the fullness of my calling and destiny! I accept the power of the woman You have created me to be! I will not live quietly; I roar with the excellence and authority you have given me from this day forward!"

"In the mighty name of Jesus, Amen!"

CHOKED

Struck by a curveball (PTSD) it came out of nowhere Post-Traumatic Stress Disorder
Sometimes known as Shell Shock; Flashbacks; Bad dreams; Frightening thoughts and Nightmares
Soldiers involved in combat suffer from a traumatic event.

A highly trained Assassin built like a capital "Y" was a master in his craft and a member of the Special Forces Unit in the United States Army. He often said, "I never missed a target". With that being said, I was completely turned on by this skilled sharpshooter profession. Especially, the way he targeted me. Bullseye!

I always felt protected and respected, and very well pleased, which enhanced my love for him. My forever friend. He'd inspired me in so many ways. He helped me to smile more and had me laughing quite often. He encouraged me to let go and let God deal with things I cannot control. A real gentleman that knows how to treat a lady. Besides, that's the nickname he gave me "Lady". I moved in with him (should have known better), but we enjoy being together. And Yes, most definitely, the married type; communicates very well; is a great listener; faithful; and when he prays, you feel the anointing. That's when my soul opened up. I knew he was the man for me. Plus, he had me spoiled rotten ever since we met. Our friendship was solid as a rock.

After a couple of years of living together, I began to witness signs of PTSD. On some occasions, he reminisced about being a sniper. Oftentimes, he will fall asleep watching some type of Army channel. I had difficulty sleeping hearing the sounds of rapid gunfire, hand grenades and bombs exploding, and sounds of Helicopters and Airplanes flying. I had to find the remote to turn the TV off. I'm quite certain these sounds gave him flashbacks. In fact, he attacked me twice while sleeping.

One night, I was awakened with his hand over my mouth, saying in my ear, "Shhh, be quiet, don't scream, I'm protecting you from the enemy." I was able to wake him up wiggling by body, removing his hand, and screaming his name for him to snap out of it. Then he came to himself. That startled both of us. It was around 4:00 a.m. We couldn't go back to sleep. We stayed up drinking coffee and listening to Wendell B.

Approximately 3 weeks had gone by since the second episode occurred. I had a very long and busy day. I worked and went to class that night earning a Master's. I was exhausted. I just wanted to get home take a shower and go straight to bed. Not knowing, there was a surprise waiting for me on the other side of that door. I walked into a dream. Dinner on the stove. Candles lit throughout the house with a selection of smooth groves playing in the background. It was all good. And having a massage put me straight to sleep. I was knocked out, once my head hit the pillow.

Sometime later during the night, I had trouble breathing. I'm awakened by him choking me, trying to kill the enemy. He had a hold of my grown, choking me around my neck, and leaving a ring around my neck. I know God sent His Angels to save me. I was able to wrestle with him, screaming his name. He finally snapped out of it. Then he came to himself. I was scared to death. I got up crying and went into the other bedroom. He enters the room being very sympathetic. Feeling ashamed saying, " I couldn't live with myself if I had accidentally killed you." We talked about him having signs of PTSD, and there should be help available for retired veterans who have nightmares from traumatic events and reliving them.

Also, there should be benefits available for PTSD being considered a work-related illness. We also discussed my moving out because it wasn't safe for me anymore. After all of that, I still wanted to stay and help him get cured. I even suggested staying in separate bedrooms. But he was still afraid of harming me. We both agreed it was for the best that I move out. We remain great friends. He sought the help he needed, receiving compensation for PTSD and he's doing well. Praise God! You can't keep a good man down.

MOTHER OF DRUG ADDICTED SON

Be selective about the company you keep. They can drag you down. "Do not be misled: Bad company corrupts good character" (1 Cor 15:33 NIV).
I will focus on the positive that recovery is possible.

My son, Ronnie, needed help. He relapsed again. It's a process for him to get clean and stay clean. He would get off the drugs and back on the drugs. From not drinking alcohol to back to drinking alcohol. This is an emotional roller coaster. I know he's devastated that it happened again, and I am too. I would tell him to "change the people in your circle. The company you keep influences your conduct." It's obvious what I say goes in one ear and out the other. He must want to change more than I do for him. However, I will not verbalize my negative thinking.

Unbelievably, his Dad and I had gotten to a place where we would rather he be locked up, instead of being on these streets. At least, we know his whereabouts and have a good night's sleep. Every time we hear on the news about another black man being found dead, we often wonder if that could be Ronnie because it's been a few weeks or so since we last heard from him. He has found a job, so I let him use my car, to get back and forth to work. Sometime later my car was found vandalized; shot up with bullet holes. A total loss. He was nowhere to be found. Being full of anxiety, I didn't know if he was dead or alive.

During that time I was receiving inpatient physical therapy at Frazier Rehab. While there, I constantly prayed for my son. Asking God to forgive our sins; to take care of Ronnie; give him a touch of Your favor; send Your Angels to cover and protect him. Also, thank God for offering His grace and mercy. In the mighty name of Jesus, Amen. Immediately, I felt God's peace, when I let go of the load. I will hold onto my faith, and wait on the Lord. God can make what seems impossible possible. He's a miracle-working God.

Finally, Ronnie calls. But the addictive behavior continues. He has to admit to himself that his life is unmanageable. He has to turn it over to a higher power, than himself; what I understood to be the "first step" in recovery. I continue to pray with boldness asking God to deliver him again, from these addictions. Ronnie needs to learn how to receive God's mercy. Letting go of guilt and shame. I will keep believing that recovery is possible. I'm aware that he had several setbacks, but God's mercy is bigger than any mistakes we've made. There is a purpose to his addiction. I received a letter from my son releasing the pain he held within. He writes:

"Dear Mama, this story isn't like most stories you hear. My name is Ronnie McWhorter from Louisville, Kentucky, the Bluegrass state. Where you find, Pimps, Hustlers, and Kingpins. From where I have been all these names sound great. But, since I'm older, these names have changed, quite a bit. Through all my ups and downs, my friends, loved ones, and anyone who has come in contact with this soul of a man have been disappointed and let down. Nothing good has happened to me, except having my son, JaCarie.

Above all, he's the one that I let down the most. I'm lost, with no means of finding my way to dry land. I was drowning in my pool of pain and self-pity. And having a self-imposed crisis, from the action I put forth. On this day 12-11-2018, something happens, and everything in my life changed. Not only was it my Mama's birthday, but I found the power to go on. Here's my story about finding power.

As far as I can remember, I never thought I was good enough. It wasn't because I wasn't getting love from my family. I always felt like something was missing. So, I live through other people's accomplishments. Daydreaming and wishing they were mine, hoping that one day my luck would change. Hopefully, it happens soon. But that thought soon sailed away and wouldn't return for many years.

As a young man, I went through many depressing days. I wasn't even a teenager yet when I had my first drink. Safe to say I didn't like it, but everyone in school was doing it. I just wanted to fit in, so I did it, too. But, that didn't last too long, because I was introduced to weed. That day my whole life changed.

Everything that made me sad, angry, depressed, or afraid went away. I felt like that was the missing piece I was looking for been found. This feeling only lasted for 30 minutes to an hour. Then I went back to that lonely, afraid, little boy, that I hated. I had to find myself again. Then I vowed, that I wouldn't go another day without it. My mother and father had no idea what I was going through. They only saw what I allowed them to see. I lied, cheated, and even stole to stay high because I never wanted to feel that pain I felt before, to enter my body again. I could hide it pretty well.

Back then, weed was so cheap. Never in a million years did I think I had a problem. However, this went on for several years, until I had my first encounter with (LMPD) Louisville Metro Police. At the time, I was 17 years old. I figured they would slap me on my wrist, and put me in Rehab.

Also, my first encounter with AA (alcohol anonymous) was in 1999, at a place called "Ten Brook". The kids there were well-off and ungrateful. Their parents were doctors and lawyers. These kids were doing drugs I never heard of before such as Heroin and Meth. I was like, "What the hell is that?" I'm thinking to myself, I only do weed. If I had parents as doctors and lawyers I wouldn't even smoke cigarettes. I was in so much denial that I couldn't even stop smoking weed to pass the urine test, we had every Wednesday. I found a way to cheat the test and did it very well. Even graduated from the program faster than everyone else, by lying and cheating. Not knowing, that what I was doing, will bite me in the ass, later on.

It wasn't long after leaving the program that I found Cocaine. From then on, me and her (cocaine) would be together. The things I've done to keep her around, were so bad, that my whole personality changed. To the point where, I went from being happy with what weed did for me, to hating everyone, and everything. I didn't know why at time, but I never thought it was cocaine. I only wanted to be noticed when I started getting high.

Then, I only wanted peace. Something cocaine wouldn't allow me to have. She (cocaine), took all the ambitions that I obtain through other people's accomplishments, to only wanting her, and nothing else. So, for the next 20 years, I would be going in and out of rehab, and in and out of prison. Losing friends loved ones, and several material things didn't matter to me, anyway. My whole life was in shambles. I was so far down, there was nowhere else to go, but up.

I met so many people on this journey. But there's one who stands out more than anyone else. That said something to me, that made a whole lot of sense. "How powerless my life is; is how unmanageable my living was? To me, he looks like a man with all the answers. So, I had a question for him. "How do I find that power?" All my life I've done nothing but things that would take me further from the Man, I know that can fix our problems.

When I think back, it was at the beginning, I said there was always something missing. I never would believe something that I couldn't see would be able to fix me. It was hard for me to get over that hurdle. The pain had gotten so great that I was willing to believe in anything. This man God sent into my life showed me how to pray, and he showed me what willingness was. I'm truly grateful that God didn't give up on me with all I've done. He's given me another chance, a new start, another beginning. And I can't wait to see, what else God has in store for me. This power is accessible to you, only if you believe in a power greater than you. May God bless you, Ronnie.

"We all face disappointments and setbacks, but if we're going to see God's best, we have to have a bounce-back mentality. That means when you get knocked down, you don't stay down. You get back up again. You have to know that every time adversity comes against you, it's a setup for a comeback" (Joel Osteen).

Presently, Ronnie is clean and following a program that will keep his focus on staying clean and sober, day by day. We have to take our burdens to the Lord and leave them there. Don't be in bondage to anything. "Be alert and of sober mind. Be self-controlled and watchful.

Your adversary, the devil, prowls around like a roaring lion looking for someone to devour" (1 Peter 5:8 NIV). We're called to be attentive and alert because we have a real enemy lurking around. If your life is ineffective and depressed or unproductive and stagnant, look at the people you surrounded. Misery loves company, so steer clear of negative-thinking people. They will drag you down with them.

I will keep standing in the gap praying for my son. I pray that he renews his mind with the Word of God. It will change his life for the better, help him think with faith, and not be in fear, with assurance, instead of anxiety, and be full of joy, instead of negativity. I trust God will bring him through whatever storms he's facing. I believe God is watching over my son and will bless him in a mighty way. God has a way to make miracles out of our mistakes, He's so full of mercy. Besides, it is the goodness of God, that leads you to repentance.

"You can have a solid foundation by building your life around the Word of God. By doing so, we would be able to withstand any storms that beat against us. After hearing the Word and not obeying or putting it into practice is like a foolish man who built his house on sand. Therefore, when the storms come into our lives, we will fall with a great crash" (Matt 7:24-27 NIV).

CONFUSED

Have you ever watched your loved one deteriorate?
Were you ever forced to imagine things that aren't really there?
Have you ever been frustrated and so upset, you needed to take deep breaths, counting to 10?
Maybe you had to leave out the room, so your loved one won't see you crying.

Mama moved in with me a couple of years later, after my Dad died. There were early signs of Alzheimer's but it appeared to be gradual, thinking her constant repeating was due to her age. She kept saying over and over and over again, "I want to go home. I want to go home. I want to go home", but she was already at home. To keep peace and Mama's anxiety down, I told several fibs. I must admit, I wasn't very honest about staying in her world. She would often ask me to call Jesse, her husband, and my father, to come to get her, but he's deceased. So, I just stayed in her world saying, "He's on his way". There were times, we laughed and talked about things she enjoyed doing with her sister. Quite often, she'll call me her name thinking I'm she.

One afternoon returning home from Dialysis, Mama fell and broke her right hip. Following surgery, she was placed in rehab, becoming a resident at the long-term care facility, directly across the street from my Condo. It was very convenient. Plus, she settled in nicely. Many of the patients there were demented. While there, her demented rambling continues showing symptoms of Alzheimer's disease a common form of Dementia. We could tell the disease was progressing and eventually diagnosed with the illness. She was presently receiving Dialysis 3 days a week for End Stage Renal Disease (ESRD). From that day on, right before my eyes, I saw death at work, my mother deteriorating right in front of me.

No matter how tearful our paths may be, and no matter what kind of adversity we encounter. We can always find something to thank God for, and we have so many reasons to worship God in song singing His praises. Mama had more good days than bad. She was strong in the Lord and steady in her faith, which encouraged me to trust God more. Quietly she said, "I'm on Cloud 9. I feel like floating because God loves me. I'm never alone, he's always with me, and all is well." During those times, Mom and I had some of the best conversations about how she felt relaxed, being in her world. I feel good because I was honoring my beautiful mother, the one I love the most. And, she's happy.

While at the facility, Mama was the peacemaker. She displayed humility and kindness. She made friends with Ernestine, Pearl, and Louise. These women were in their 70's and 80's but act as if they were in their 50's and 60's. These queens were fabulous. They had exquisite taste in clothes. Wore beautiful Pajamas, Gowns, and Kaftans. Including, pearls around their necks and bracelets on their arms. I can tell these women lived lavishly. So I made sure my mama was elegant too. Mama was very fond of these women and their families. And they loved her too.

On many occasions, Mama thought these women were crazy, because half the time, they act like they didn't have good sense. She said, "I am talking about one thing, and they be talking about something else." That made me crack up laughing, cause half the time, Mama acts the same way when she's with me. I guess they are in their world together. Friends with Alzheimer's & Dementia disease.

I met Pearl at a Talent show in the facilities Dining room singing to someone she thought was her man. She had a beautiful voice. I guess her mind went back to the past when she sang in nightclubs. During the intermission, she approached this man, the guy she kept her eyes on while singing. Asking him, "Who is she?" "You need to let her know who I am." He said, "This is my wife, so who are you?" Pearl responded, "Hi my name is Pearl and I'm very sorry. He looks just like my man." I could only assume, it was her illness, that caused the flashback. She felt he really was her man.

I met Louise at a Potluck in the facility's Dining Room. It was Family and Friends Day. Louise was a gorgeous lady, with long silky Platinum gray hair. She talked about cooking all the time. She started cooking at a very young age. She always helped her mother and grandma in the kitchen. She states people loved when she cooked and look forward to eating her food. Louise had three husbands, and they all died. She often feels lonely. She wants a companion to spend time with. She always had someone in her life. A family member shared that, "she was overwhelmingly affected when her mom didn't know who she was anymore. Louise craves for human contact and is glad she made friends at the facility.

I also met Dorothy at Family and Friends Day. She and Louise were roommates. Mama didn't care too much for Dorothy. She said "Dorothy acts like she is racist. Thinking she's better than anyone else. She thinks she's so important." One day, Mama saw her turning up her nose at one of the CNAs (certified nurse assistants). She was being hateful and talked down to them. Mama mentioned, "You can be talking about something, then Dorothy twists the conversation around making it all about herself." Does that remind you of somebody?

Ernestine was Mama's roommate. She reminded me of Mrs. Chancellor that played on "The Young and The Restless". She was the oldest of them all, very elegant. Always upbeat and very energetic. She was into crafts and kept the room decorative. But Ernestine did not participate in Sunday morning activities, because she did not believe in God. And she too didn't like black being around people, until she met and became friends with my mother. Ms. Ernestine said Emma is the "FIRST BLACK FRIEND she ever had and who also told her about the LORD." From the very first time I met Ms. Ernestine, I thought she was a handful. When Mama first introduce us, I said, "Hello Ms. Ernestine." She said, "Hi bitch." Mama said, "Don't pay her no mind. Ernestine doesn't have it all. She's crazy, especially when you don't believe in God, just look over her". "I said Mama, she can hear you". Mama goes on to say, "She's hard of hearing. And went on to say, " I'm trying to tell you, she is hard of hearing. She can't hear well, I have to holler at her all the time. I'm telling you Ernestine can't hear". I said, "Mama, Ms. Ernestine is either ignoring you or the volume needs to be turned up because she's wearing a Hearing Aid. Mama whispered, "I think she's a lunatic and she's hard of hearing.

If you don't know the Lord, never attended church and never studied the Bible. No wonder the Beast inside you attacks and acts out. Now you're attacking others. There's no self-control or self-discipline. When you spend time with God, hearts change; transformation takes place; you grow spiritually; become humble, kind, empathetic, and show compassion.

One day, Ms. Ernestine waited for her son, but he never showed up. She became very upset, bringing her to tears. Mama uses the opportunity to talk about the goodness of God saying that "He will never leave you or forsake you. You are never alone. His Holy Spirit lives in you. He loves you unconditionally. He fully paid for your sins, died on the cross and He arose again. And He blessed you and your family financially. All good gifts come from the Lord. Believe in the Lord Jesus, and you will be saved. That day, Ms. Ernestine smiled, accepting Jesus Christ as her personal Lord & Savior.

Oftentimes, Ms. Ernestine looks very stunning. No matter what, she stayed dolled up. She wore the most luxurious robes and the prettiest Kaftans, and her jewelry glittered and shines brightly across the room. She dressed like and smelled like money. On occasions, I noticed Ms. Ernestine's generosity. She would bless the CNAs with gifts she didn't want that be given to her. And she would hand out cash tips when something extra was done for her.

After a couple of years, Mama's health started failing. She no longer needed dialysis. It wasn't doing her any good because her blood pressure kept dropping. Later, placed in hospice care. I witnessed the love each girlfriend showed my Mama during her last days. My heart was full of compassion for these women watching their friend Emma, my precious mother, leave this world and be with my father.

Before my mother slept away, she screamed for my Dad to come to get her. She yelled out, "Jesse open the door and let me in." It was a few days later on 2-10-2014 when Mama reunited with my father.

41

He passed away on 09-28-2009. They were married for 61 years. We were truly blessed have to some amazing parents. They loved us unconditionally. We miss them so much. Continue watching over us Mama and Daddy and rest in peace, along with my baby girl, Demetra. We love you guys. From your children Pierre, Carlos and me.

UNLOADING

Are you willing to trust God in your circumstances? Do you believe that no problem is beyond God's power?

Trusting God means looking beyond what we can see to what God sees. God is the Lord who is strong and mighty. He is of great power, the ONLY One abundant in strength. All power belongs to Him. Nothing is beyond God's power. Begin again to pray, sing praises keeping the faith. God is in control, and all power is in His hands. Even in the worst situations, God is worthy of our praise. Surely, God is going to bless me. Surely means without a doubt, truly believing, convinced that God will bless you. Don't be moved by negativity, don't get discouraged by what seems to be impossible, and stop complaining about how long it's taken God's timing is perfect. He's always right on time.

Are there any gay people in your family?

There are several in my family. My daughter, nephew, cousin, and close friend are gay. That was hard for me to accept at first because of my beliefs. But who I am to judge? Is that Christ-like? Thanks be to God that He is no respecter of persons. For God so loved the world, and He loves every person equally. We are called to do likewise. Jesus calls us to maturity; not to discriminate. Let go of judgment. LGBTQ Community faces discrimination in their personal lives, in public, in the workplace, and even in church. This forces individuals to remain in the closet, guarding the secrets of who they are, in order to have some peace. This may cause mental, physical, and emotional harm.

In the words of RuPaul, an American drag queen "Be fierce; be unapologetic; be the best version of who you are; be authentic. If you can't love yourself how in the hell are you gonna love somebody else? Can I get an AMEN up in here?"

Do you need to reposition yourself?

Bishop T.D. Jakes asks in his book (Reposition Yourself), "Can you have a heart for something that is not about yourself? Being stubborn has you stuck. Being selfish has you stuck. You are the gift. Your story is your gift. Your history is your destiny. Your success is in your struggle."

"You buy what you want and then find yourself out there struggling for what you need. How foolish is that? You cannot correct what you will not confront. We must be strategic and deliberate. Our punches must connect. We must fight strategically for the prizes we long to enjoy. We must invest our energy indirect connections to our goals. No story without a struggle."

Are you disappointed?

Friend, I come to inspire, motivate and encourage you to be all you can be, with your unique self. There is no one in the world like you. God, our Architect, designs us, and He didn't make any mistakes. Be okay with who you are, I encourage you to hold on to your faith in God. Develop a grateful heart. Believe in His power. Trust Him. Always give Him thanks. Be still and know; God is in control, ordering your steps, and He's working everything out for your good.

Are you overwhelmed by the pressures of responsibility?

"Whenever God is getting ready to promote you, there will always be an escalation of troubles. When you turn your eyes on the Lord, you begin to focus on His blessing, His favor, and His anointing for your life. As you change your focus from your problems to His power, you will find that you have to be grateful to be victorious" (Bishop T.D. Jakes).

You cannot win what you are unable to face such as fear of failure. When you attempt something you've never done before, or previously failed at, it's normal to feel afraid. Experiencing failure is the price you must pay to achieve success.

You can't get stronger if you are not under pressure. In doing the thing you fear to do, that's when your confidence grows.

Also, being fearful keeps us from fulfilling any vision God may have given us. Step out and take a risk-based on faith trusting God for success. Tough times don't last. Tough people do. Never count God out no matter how things look. Obey the Lord, and don't be surprised when the blessings come. Be extremely grateful.

Are you feeling drained after having great success?

Release. Let go of the load. Put your trust in God, our Great Physician, He will make you whole again.

Are you depressed because somebody walked out on you?

For every challenge that can show up in someone's life, there is a spiritual solution. Let them go! Quit being sour because somebody walked out and left you. Let them go! God is the best choice to be free from depression. You don't need anybody who doesn't want you. There is someone perfectly designed just for you.

And what are you thinking? If you change your thinking, you can change how you feel. The devil is after your destiny. Depression is a tool Satan uses to keep the Will of God from your life. The Word of God is the tool God uses to change the way of thinking to bring success in your life. When we put our trust in God and begin to praise Him, depression lifts and hope is restored. But we constantly go elsewhere looking for substitutes trying to replace God (pornography, social media, drugs, alcohol, sex, gambling, shopping, and eating).

Are you going through a storm?

I can say with great confidence He is a God in the storm. It may be uncomfortable, but He's our Protector always ready to help in times of trouble and He will not abandon you. Let go of the load, and release the pain within. Surrender all to God. There is a reason for the storm. At some point, we will face tests and trials. They show us who we truly are. We must pray, persevere, focus on God, and develop a deeper faith. Storms have a way of bringing things together for our good. Plus builds character making people better.

Have you ever been let down?

Be encouraged! Everyone needs some type of encouragement. People crave it. It gives confidence. When circumstances and difficulties repeatedly play in your mind, remember your victories from the past, that'll encourage you, and then strength begins to rise in your heart.

Have you replaced God?

Make Him a priority. Put God first in your life and bring Him honor. Begin giving thanks the moment you wake up. Focus on Him throughout the day. Pray. Spend time daily reading the Scriptures and meditating on His Word. "For where your treasure is, there your heart will be also." (Matt 6:21 NIV)

Do you need peace?

Be the peace you seek. Nobody can bring you peace but yourself. When someone is mean or angry with you hold on to your peace. You be an Eagle and rise above it, even when you feel yourself getting annoyed and frustrated. Watch out for the bait. Cease from strife and take the high road. Do your best to be at peace with others, even if they don't take your peace. You move on. Hurt feelings and unforgiveness will rob you of receiving God's blessings. Nothing is worth losing your peace over. Even though you get tired, persevere. God sees all, and He will see you through in the midst of it all. So do the right thing no matter what's happening, God will fight your battles and will reward you. "But in that coming day, no weapon turned against you will succeed. You will silence every voice raised to accuse you. The servants of the Lord enjoy these benefits; their vindication will come from me. I, the Lord have spoken!" (Isa 54:17 NLT).

Do you have bold faith? What would you do for a friend?

In Mark chapter 2, is an example of having bold faith. There are a group of friends putting their faith in action for a paralyzed friend. These "tear off the roof team" had a situation only Jesus alone can fix. They heard Jesus had come home. So while still in bed, they took their disabled friend to see Jesus. But, when they got there the door was blocked by a crowd of people wanting to see Jesus. It didn't matter; the friends got creative. They went to the rooftop of the house and tore out a hole in the roof, big enough to lower the bed down in the presence of Jesus to be healed. When Jesus saw the boldness of their faith, He immediately and publicly healed their paralyzed friend. He got out of bed from a paralyzed state and walked. People were all amazed witnessing the miracle-working power of Jesus. A true friend, a real friend, a biblical friend "loves at all times" (Proverbs 17:17 NIV). To my dearest friends, you have a friend in me.

Friend, I pray that you are encouraged, and just for today remember the goodness of Jesus, giving Him thanks for the things He did for you in the past, and the things He will do for you in the future.

LYRICS IN MY HEART

Lord I can't take it
Help me make it
What do I do
What shall I do
Must run to You

Got to keep on running to You
Can't stop; won't stop running
Got to keep on running; running
Can't stop; won't stop running;
Got to keep on running to You

Father what am I supposed to do
Can't handle this without You
Please show me what I need to do
Waiting patiently for You

Is there something else I need to do
Just surrender all to You
Waiting patiently for You
Now running to You

Got to keep on running to You
Can't stop; won't stop running
Got to keep on running; running
Can't stop; won't stop running
Got to keep on running to You

Kept running falling and stumbling
I lost my way looking back

Hoping you direct my path
Help get me back on track

I got to keep on running
Keep running; don't stop running
Keep running; can't stop running
Keep running; won't stop running

You turn my messes into miracles
I believe you can do the impossible
Things are better all around me
You purified and strengthen me

Got to keep on running to you
Won't stop; can't stop running to You

HE WALKS WITH ME

Can you picture yourself taking a long walk with God admiring the breathtaking creation he had made while holding his hand? The park is exquisite with rainbow colors throughout. You're holding His hands and sharing every detail of your life, "things He already knew, before He formed you in your mother's womb" (Jere 1:5 NIV). You begin to focus, concentrate, and listen; quieting your soul to hear what the Spirit has to say. Naturally, start giving God glory, honor, and praise along the way. Since I'm walking with the Word I must speak the Word to the Word.

"In the beginning was the Word, and the Word was with God and the Word was truly God" (John 1:1 NIV).

At an early age, I attended church school and one thing I always remembered was that Jesus is the Word made flesh; "holy one son of God" (Luke 1:35 NIV) and "a friend that sticks closer than a brother" (Pr. 18:24 NIV).

It's a privilege and honor to say, "I am a friend of God" He calls me a friend. Walking with the Lord will be like walking with my dearest and closest friend whom I call my sister. I truly adore and cherish my sister-friends, with whom I share my deepest feelings and some of my secrets.

Some things are only kept between me and God. Our greatest concern is getting our needs met, but God's greatest concern is developing our faith. "Without faith, it is impossible to please God" (Heb. 11:6 NIV).

Being blessed and highly favored walking with God I cannot "let my heart be troubled nor let it be afraid" (John 14:27 NIV). That gives me peace in every circumstance and courage and strength for every challenge.

I can rest assured that the Lord knows what is best for me. "For I know the plans I have for you, declares the Lord, plans to prosper you and not to harm you, plans to give you hope and a future" (Jer. 29:11 NIV).

My burdens are too much to carry, but there is nothing I'm going through that I cannot cast on the Lord. "Cast your burden upon the Lord and He will sustain you; He will never let the righteous fall" (Ps. 55:22 NIV).

God loves me so much that He delivered me from a low place. Thinking I would never walk again I began to lose all hope, "He reached down from on high and took hold of me" (Psalm 18:16 NIV). And then the Word reminded me, " If you believe all things are possible to him who believes" (Mark 9:23 NIV). I cried out saying, "Lord I do believe; help me with my unbelief!" (Mark9:24 NIV)

Father, thank You for never giving up on me. You see all. Nothing is hidden from You. You waited for me to draw nearer to you and I'm so grateful. Help me to encourage others who feel overburdened. Help me to trust in You when circumstances feel overwhelming. Thank You for helping me rise up through adversities. Thank You for Your goodness and for being so faithful. I will continue to walk in obedience and not step out from under your protection. Thank You for restoring health unto me. Thank You for being behind the scene and working things out for my good. I believe I will see Your power in new ways. I declare by faith I've been redeemed. In the Name of Jesus, Lord it's been a mighty good day.

CONCLUSION

Life happens. Every time you turn around something happens. If it's not one thing it's another. Too many hardships to overcome, but don't turn back now though, keep moving forward. Even when you dealing with drug and alcohol addictions; burying a loved one shot by a stray bullet; a child being bullied at school; caring for an aging parent; facing a severe medical condition; mental illness; job loss; facing retirement but still have to work; eviction; homelessness; divorce; trunk load of bills; unfair treatment; racism; police brutality; suicide; domestic violence; LGBTQ community still fighting for their rights; wrongful conviction unlawful imprisonment; the list goes on and on, but there's hope, God will see you through. The Word of God tells us "No weapon formed against you shall prosper" (Isa 54:17 NKJV); "The battle is the Lord, and he will give all of you into our hands" (1 Sam 17:47). We got the victory.

Some trials or adversities we face are a test of our faith. We learn perseverance and a deeper relationship with God. "because we know suffering produces perseverance; perseverance, character; and character, hope" (Rom 5:3-4 NIV).

Don't get discouraged if nothing happens, even if it's been a while after you have prayed. Quite often, continue to persevere. God waits to act on purpose. So when He turns that problem around there won't be any doubt that it was His power that made way where there was no way.

"Wait for the Lord; be strong and take heart and wait for the Lord" (Ps. 27:14 NIV).

"The prayer of a righteous man is powerful and effective" (James 5:16 NIV). God is in control. There is absolutely nothing more powerful than God. He has all power in His hands. Our faith, confidence, and trust are in God only. Therefore, wherever we are God is and all is well with my soul.

Release the pain held within. Let go of the load. Have that even now faith. Don't be discouraged to give up on God. Get your passion back. Sometimes that's the only time we learn is while we are in the struggle, or while we are in the wilderness. Still, we have victory in Jesus who causes us to triumph. When you have a relationship with God, you will experience His peace, goodness, and favor. You don't have to live in self-pity. God will never lose His power.

Remember, every good and perfect gift comes from the Lord. He knows what's best for us. If you only believe you will see the goodness of God. It's according to your faith. Don't let what you see affect what you say. God can take what's broken and make it perfect. He can mend things back together again. Nothing can stop Him. He can bring life to a dead situation.

During difficult times, the Lord enables us to see our lives from His viewpoint and we regain hope. When I glance back to see how far I've come, I have to give Him praise. I'm grateful that I made it against all odds. Just take a minute, and look back on a past event to get a good idea of what God has already done for you. You definitely be amazed to see His goodness and faithfulness. He's always been there and will always be there for you. Every difficulty we face is an opportunity for God to flex His muscles proving He is very dependable and true to His Word. God said, "Never will I leave you; never will I forsake you" (Heb. 13:5 NIV). Have a made-up mind to keep believing, honoring, trusting, and praising God because He is worthy.

Don't let anyone's judgment or criticism determine who you are. You decide that. Get rid of negative self-talk. Be humble, kind, and compassionate. Don't murmur or complain. Jump over the hurdles that come in your life. Just keep living, everyone will be struck by a curveball. It comes out of nowhere.

Pray; "The prayer of a righteous man is powerful and effective" (James 5:16 NIV).

Be strong; "Finally, be strong in the Lord and in his mighty power" (Eph. 6:10 NIV).

Be content; "Not that I was ever in need, for I have learned how to be content with whatever I have" (Phil 4:11 NLT). You're happy and satisfied; your mind is at ease; you're not controlled by your circumstances; and giving God thanks in everything.

"Let the peace of Christ rule in your hearts, and be thankful" (Col 3:15 NIV).

"Taste and see that the Lord is good" (Ps 34:8 NIV). His goodness will multiply in your life. Thank Him while you can. Watch and see what He's about to do in your life. That is what seems impossible; when placed in God's hands He will make it possible. God is the God of the Turnaround. God can take a difficult situation, and abruptly turn it into a positive experience, that is beyond human explanation. "But as for you, you meant evil against me; but God meant it for good" (Genesis 50:20 NKJV). I don't know what kind of problem you may be going through today. If you just hold on and take your stand on the Word of God, he will turn that difficulty around for your good.

It is my prayer that Let Go of The Load restores your hope and brings you joy that only comes from God. If you stay joyful long enough, you will become happy. "The joy of the Lord is my strength" (Neh. 8:18 NLT). When we have joy, we have the strength and power to overcome every obstacle we may be facing. When we think about God's amazing grace, we have unspeakable joy that only comes from Him. The Bible makes it clear that God is "Sovereign". Resting and worship is the highest place we can be. We must learn to rest in the sovereignty of our God. He is our King and has authority and control over all things. We pray to glorify Him. Prayer is for our benefit to receive from Him. "Nothing is too hard for you" (Jer. 32:17 NIV).

We must treasure the Word of God, and we must respond by obeying and doing what it says. Develop resilience and draw on His power moment by moment. God's Word reveals our motives, exposes our flaws, rebukes our sins, and demands change. We must get to a place where we're fully persuaded to trust God. He restores hope. Definitely, experience His peace that is too impossible to describe. Without a doubt, receive unspeakable joy. Come to Him for protection and find safety.

I will close with this priestly blessing "The Lord bless you and keep you; the Lord make his face shine upon you and be gracious to you; the Lord turn his face toward you and give you peace" (Num. 6:24-26 NIV). In the Name of Jesus, Amen!

Thank You Jesus, for everything you have done and continue to do in my life!

ACKNOWLEDGMENTS

Writing this book was more rewarding than I could ever imagine. None of this would have been possible without Carlos Guevarra and the team at Citi of Books for assisting me in republishing Let Go of The Load. This book is a tool to encourage, entertain, and uplift spirits. I'm so grateful Let Go of The Load received another opportunity to touch hearts and renew minds worldwide. Thank you for believing in me and giving my story recognition.

To my family; To my husband Charlie: Honey you have stuck by me from the very beginning of my disability. I appreciate you and am so very grateful God bless me with you. Thank you for loving, caring, and supporting me the way you do.

To my daughter RayRay: My favorite girl. You are very special to me. I am so blessed that God saw fit to bless me to have you. I appreciate you so much. Thank you for loving and caring for me. Be great in all you do.

To my son Ronnie: My favorite son. You are very special to me. I am blessed to see how God is transforming you in ways we didn't think would be possible. Keep up the good work. Thank you for your love and for looking out for me.

To my grandchildren: JaCarie, Kaivon, Kyeli: You guys are my Emmy, Grammy, Oscar, and Tony (EGOT) Awards. Be Successful. Granny loves you so much and thank you for the love you have for me.

To my great-granddaughter Saraiya: RiRi, baby girl you bring GiGi so much joy. I love you more than words can say. You will always be my little princess and most definitely my (EGOT).

To my brothers: Pierre and Carlos: I love you guys for always having my back. Mama & Daddy would be so proud of both of you.

To my sister Mousie: Sis you are an inspiration. Thank you for always uplifting my spirit.

To my big sister-cousin Norma Jean: for always being the person I could turn to during those dark and painful days. Jean you sustained me in ways that I never knew I needed. Thank you, GiGi.

To my Prayer line family: Pastor Carl Garmon Sr, First lady Janice, Sister Tasha, Brothers Joseph & Carl Jr., and fellow members. Thank you guys for blessing me with the Word of God every morning since 2016. My faith has strengthened. My hunger for the Word increased. Now I pray bold prayers. God hears me and He answers me. You guys are truly a blessing in my life. Thank you for keeping me in your thoughts and prayers.

To the rest of my family from the late Emma (Tee) & Jesse Curd: Thank you for supporting me I love you guys.

To all my sister-friends: God blessed me with some amazing Earth Angels that keeps me uplifted, entertained, and looking glamorous. I don't know what I would do without you, beautiful Queens. You have been so good to me. I'm grateful to have you all in my life. I pray you all to be blessed abundantly.

To my Thoroughbreds, I'll always love you.